HAZARD

RULES

Hi, pleased to meet you.

We hope you enjoy our book about Eden Hazard!

DAN

THIS IS A WELBECK CHILDREN'S BOOK
Published in 2020 by Welbeck Children's Books Limited
An imprint of the Welbeck Publishing Group
20 Mortimer Street, London W1T 3JW
Text, design and illustration © Welbeck Publishing Limited 2020
ISBN: 978-1-78312-538-8

Writer: Simon Mugford
Designer and Illustrator: Dan Green
Design manager: Emily Clarke
Executive Editor: Suhel Ahmed
Production: Rachel Burgess

A catalogue record for this book is available from the British Library.

Printed in the UK
10 9 8 7 6 5 4 3 2 1

Statistics and records correct as of March 2020

FOOTBALL SUPERSTARS

HAZARD

RULES

SIMON MUGFORD   DAN GREEN

CONTENTS

CHECK OUT THE NUMBERS TO SEE HOW GOOD HAZARD IS:

2 ...Premier League wins

1 ...FA Cup win

2 ...Europa League wins

1 ...Ligue 1 Championship

3 ...Player's Player of the Year Awards

352

appearances and

110

. . . goals for Chelsea

Estimated

£90 MILLION

. . . transfer to Real Madrid

More than

26 MILLION

. . . Instagram followers

HAZARD I.D.

NAME: *Eden Michael Hazard*

DATE OF BIRTH: *7 January 1991*

PLACE OF BIRTH: *La Louvière, Belgium*

HEIGHT: *1.75 m*

POSITION: *Winger / attacking midfielder / forward*

CLUBS: *Lille, Chelsea, Real Madrid*

NATIONAL TEAM: *Belgium*

LEFT OR RIGHT-FOOTED: *Both*

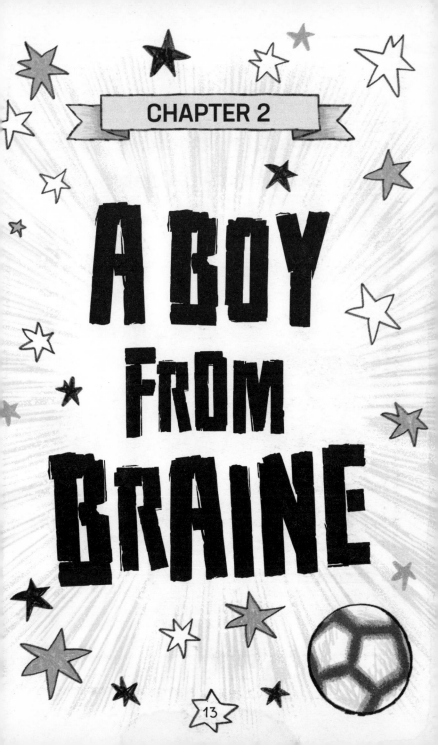

Eden Hazard was born in **1991** in the city of La Louvière in **Belgium.** He grew up in the town of **Braine-le-Comte**, with his mum, dad and three younger brothers.

The whole family were

CRAZY

about football.

Carine
(Mum)

Thierry
(Dad)

Thorgan
(Brother)

Ethan
(Brother)

Kylian
(Brother)

Eden

15

Thierry Hazard was a semi-professional footballer in the **Belgian Second Division.** He was a defender.

16

Carine Hazard played as a striker in the **Belgian Women's First Division.**

Carine only stopped playing when she was pregnant with Eden!

TEAM HAZARD

Eden

Thorgan
plays for
Borussia Dortmund

Kylian
plays for Cercle Brugge

Ethan
*youth player at
Royal Stade Brainois*

SAY 'CHEESE!'

Eden's family lived right next to their local football club **Royal Stade Brainois.**

Young Eden would **sneak** through a gap in the fence to go and **play on the pitch!**

"HE WAS AN ASTONISHING TALENT . . . HE WOULD LISTEN TO WHAT YOU TOLD HIM, BUT YOU COULDN'T REALLY TEACH HIM ANYTHING."

Pascal Delmoitiez, general manager, Royal Stade Brainois

Soon after he was **caught sneaking** onto their pitch, **Eden** began playing for Royal Stade Brainois.

Eden was one of the **smallest players** in the team, but he was **fast** and **very skilful.**

Some big Belgian clubs like **Anderlecht** and **Standard Liege** soon heard about the young star.

BOP!

But Eden stayed close to home and joined **AFC Tubize,** where his dad had played.

Eden loved watching football on TV. His **biggest idol** when he was a boy was the French midfield legend **Zinedine Zidane**.

"THERE WAS SOMETHING ABOUT HIM [EDEN], APART FROM NATURAL ABILITY, THAT TOLD ME HE WAS GOING TO THE VERY TOP."

Fathi Ennabli, Eden's coach at Tubize.

30

CHAPTER 4

BONJOUR LILLE

In **2005,** when Eden was **14**, he joined the academy at the top French side, **Lille.** Eden lived there with the other **academy players,** practising and playing football **every day!**

Thorgan and Kylian were happy for their brother, but a bit jealous, too!

Sometimes, the coaches thought Eden seemed a bit **lazy** in training.

But Eden always **showed** off his **awesome skills** when he wanted to!

Eden signed a **professional contract** with Lille in *MAY 2007*.

He started the following season in the

under–18 and **reserve** teams. Eden made his

first–team debut as a substitute in a league

match against **Nancy** in **November 2007**.

Eden became a regular in the first team in the ***2008-09 SEASON***.

In **September**, Lille were losing **2-1** at home to **Auxerre**. Eden came on as a substitute and quickly scored his **first senior goal!** Lille went on to win **3-2**.

At the end of his first full season at Lille, Eden won the

Player's Young Player of the Year Award.

EDEN'S 2008-09 RECORD

APPEARANCES	GOALS	ASSISTS
35	6	4

CHAPTER 5

BRILLIANT BELGIAN

Eden Hazard is one of the best **PENALTY-TAKERS** in the world. One of his **tricks** is a **little step** in his run-up that **fools the keeper** into going the wrong way. **OOF!**

little step

JAN CEULEMANS 1974-1992

Ceulemans was a tall, strong and powerful player who spent **14 years** at **Club Brugge.** He reached the final of **EURO 1980** with Belgium and was their captain at the **1986 WORLD CUP.**

44

MARC WILMOTS 1987-2003

Wilmots played club football in Belgium, France and Germany and scored **28 goals** for his country. He is Belgium's top **World Cup-scorer.**

ENZO SCIFO 1983-2001

Scifo appeared at four **World Cups** for Belgium and is one of their greatest ever players. He was born in the **same town** as Hazard and was his coach at **Tubize.**

45

Hazard's speed, dribbling and playmaking skill mean he's has been compared to both **Cristiano Ronaldo** and **Lionel Messi.**

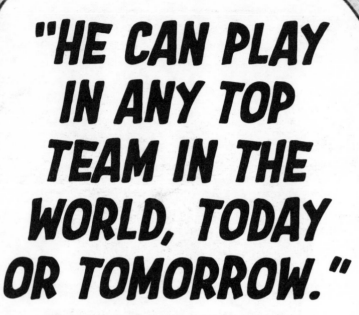

"HE CAN PLAY IN ANY TOP TEAM IN THE WORLD, TODAY OR TOMORROW."

Eden's Belgium team-mate, Vincent Kompany

CHAPTER 6

LILLE STAR

2009-10

HIGHLIGHTS OF A GREAT SEASON AT LILLE FOR EDEN.

30 JULY 2009

EUROPA LEAGUE QUALIFYING

SLOBODA UŽICE 0-2 LILLE

*Eden's first goal of the season came in this Europa League qualifier in Serbia. It was also his **first-ever** European goal!*

50

30 JANUARY 2010

LIGUE 1

LILLE 1-0 LENS

*Eden was the **hero** for Lille as his **goal** won the **Derby du Nord** against fierce local rivals, Lens.*

BOFF!

11 MARCH 2010

EUROPA LEAGUE ROUND OF 16 1ST LEG

LILLE 1-0 LIVERPOOL

*Hazard scored from a **free-kick** to record a memorable **victory** over one of the biggest teams in Europe.*

Eden won the

Player of the Month Award

for **MARCH** and the

YOUNG PLAYER OF THE YEAR AWARD

for the **second year** in a row.

He was the *first player* to *win* the Young Player of the Year Award *twice!*

EDEN'S 2009-10 RECORD

APPEARANCES	GOALS	ASSISTS
52	10	13

The **2010-11** season was a **BIG** one for Hazard and Lille. Eden's season began with a **dip in form**, but he was soon back to his **GOALSCORING** best!

BOOOM!

In **March** Eden scored an ***INCREDIBLE*** goal against **Marseille**. His left-footed shot from 35 metres out ***BLASTED*** into the net at **95 km/h!**

Eden scored **three goals** in the **Coupe de France**, including one in their **semi-final** win over **Nice**.

In the final at the **STADE DE FRANCE**, Lille beat **Paris Saint-Germain** 1-0 to win the cup for the first time in **56 YEARS!**

WHAT A WAY FOR EDEN TO WIN HIS **FIRST-EVER TROPHY!**

DOUBLE UP

In **Ligue 1**, Eden's **seven goals** and **11 assists** helped his team win their first league title since **1954**. It was Lille's first double since since **1946**.

WHAT A SEASON!

Ligue 1 Trophy

COUPE DE DAN

For his performances in **2010-11**, Eden won the **Ligue 1 Player of the Year**. It was a **FANTASTIC** end to an **AWESOME** season!

He was the youngest player ever to win the award.

And the first *Belgian!*

60

EDEN'S 2010-11 RECORD

APPEARANCES	GOALS	ASSISTS
54	12	14

2011-12

Eden wore the number 10 shirt for what would be his final season at Lille.

14 SEPTEMBER 2011

CHAMPIONS LEAGUE GROUP STAGE

LILLE 2-2 CSKA MOSCOW

*Lille's championship win meant they qualified for the **Champions League**. This was Eden's **first** appearance in the competition.*

GOAL!

3 DECEMBER 2011

LIGUE 1

AJACCIO 2-3 LILLE

*With the game tied at **2-2**, Eden came on as a substitute. In the **80th minute,** he **scored** a brilliant chipped penalty to **win the game**.*

29 APRIL 2012

LIGUE 1

LILLE 2-1 PSG

*This was a **big** game at the end of the season. Eden's 71st-minute **penalty** brought the game level, and his skilful attacking helped Lille **win 2-1!***

Hazard was **scoring more goals** than ever before! **By now**, big clubs like **Manchester United** and **Chelsea** wanted to sign him. Everyone knew that the final game of the season, against **Nancy** would be his last for Lille.

Eden scored his **first-ever first-team hat-trick** as Lille won **4-1!**

ALL OF THE FANS CLAPPED AND CHEERED HIM WHEN HE LEFT THE PITCH.

Eden was voted **Ligue 1 Player of the Year** for the second season in a row!

WHAT WOULD **HAZARD** DO NEXT?

EDEN'S RECORD AT LILLE

APPEARANCES	GOALS	ASSISTS
194	50	53

CHAPTER 7

LONDON CALLING

In the summer of 2012, Eden made up his mind. He was going to move to **London** to play for one of the **biggest clubs** in Europe:

CHELSEA.

FOOTBALL SUPERSTARS NEWS

BREAKING NEWS! Eden Hazard has signed for the **Blues!**

HAZARD A BLUE!

Chelsea had just won the **Champions League.**

Eden was joining a team with some awesome players like:

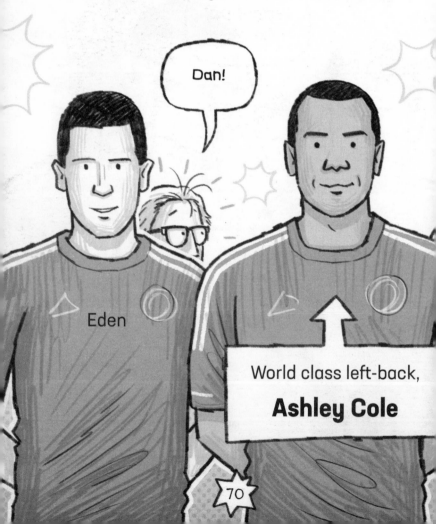

Dan!

Eden

World class left-back, **Ashley Cole**

Hazard played **_62 GAMES_** for Chelsea in his first season. He scored **13 goals** and provided **24 assists** for his team-mates.

He helped the team reach the final of the **Europa League,** but could not play himself as he was injured.

BUT EDEN DID WIN A **FIRST TROPHY** WITH CHELSEA AS THEY BEAT BENFICA 2-1.

73

PREMIER LEAGUE 2013-14

HIGHLIGHTS OF HAZARD'S SECOND SEASON WITH CHELSEA.

4 DECEMBER 2013
SUNDERLAND 3-4 CHELSEA

*Eden played brilliantly, scoring **TWO GOALS** and setting up another for Frank Lampard in this seven-goal thriller.*

8 FEBRUARY 2014

CHELSEA 3-0 NEWCASTLE

Eden scored his **first hat-trick** in the Premier League to defeat **the Magpies** at Stamford Bridge.

22 MARCH 2014

CHELSEA 6-0 ARSENAL

Eden's penalty was one of **four first-half goals** in this thrashing of Chelsea's London rivals.

75

Eden added to the awards he had

won at Lille, by winning the

PFA Young Player of the Year

and being voted

Chelsea Player of the Year.

He's gonna need a bigger cabinet!

CHAPTER 8

WORLD CLASS

Hazard played his first senior game for **Belgium** in a **friendly** against **Luxembourg** in **November 2008**. But for a time, Eden did not always get in the team.

When he was substituted in a **EURO 2012** qualifier, Eden left the stadium and was later spotted eating a burger with some friends!

But Eden loved playing for his country and was soon back in the squad.

Under manager **Marc Wilmots**, Eden became a regular in the national side. Hazard and Belgium reached the **quarter-finals** of the *2014 WORLD CUP.*

Marc Wilmots

Eden was named as **captain** for *EURO 2016* as team-mate **Vincent Kompany** was injured.

WHAT AN INCREDIBLE HONOUR!

STAR SQUAD

Eden is the captain of a talented Belgian team with lots of **awesome players**, such as:

Inter Milan striker,
Romelu Lukaku

Manchester City

midfielder,

Kevin de Bruyne

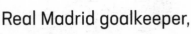
Real Madrid goalkeeper,

Thibaut Courtois

Liverpool forward,

Divock Origi

AND ME!

EDEN'S BROTHER
THORGAN

83

WORLD CUP 2018

EDEN WAS VERY HONOURED TO BE THE CAPTAIN OF HIS COUNTRY AT THE **WORLD CUP.**

23 JUNE 2018

BELGIUM 5-2 TUNISIA

Hazard scored twice in this **man-of-the-match** performance, including a **penalty** after just **SIX** minutes.

2 JULY 2018

BELGIUM 3-2 JAPAN

*Belgium were trailing 2-0 and looked to be out of the tournament, until Eden and his team-mates hit back with **THREE** goals in the last 25 minutes.*

6 JULY 2018

BRAZIL 1-2 BELGIUM

*Eden was in **sparkling** form as his team scored a famous **victory** over **Brazil** and reached the semi-finals for only the second time.*

Belgium lost the **semi–final** to **France,**

who went on to win the trophy. Eden and

Belgium beat England to finish in **third place.**

It was Belgium's **best-ever** World Cup!

HARRY KANE,
ENGLAND CAPTAIN

86

It was a **BRILLIANT** World Cup for Eden, too.

HE WAS MAN OF THE MATCH THREE TIMES.

HE SCORED THREE GOALS AND MADE TWO ASSISTS.

HE WON THE SILVER BALL AS THE SECOND-BEST PLAYER OF THE TOURNAMENT AFTER LUKA MODRIĆ.

Eden scored **FIVE** goals and provided **seven ASSISTS** to help Belgium win **ALL** of their qualifiers for **EURO 2020.**

BOOM!

EDEN'S BELGIUM RECORD

CAPS	GOALS	ASSISTS
106	32	33

CHAPTER 9

CHELSEA KING

2014-15

HIGHIGHTS OF A BIG PREMIER LEAGUE SEASON FOR HAZARD AT CHELSEA.

5 OCTOBER 2014

CHELSEA 2-0 ARSENAL

*Eden won and scored a **penalty** in this brilliant win over their London rivals.*

WAP!

BOFF!

13 DECEMBER 2014

CHELSEA 2-0 HULL

Hazard **scored** with his **head** for only the **SECOND** time in his career and provided an **assist** for Diego Costa.

3 MAY 2015

CHELSEA 1-0 CRYSTAL PALACE

Eden's goal was a **big one** - Chelsea **won** the **Premier League** title with this win!

DOUBLE DONE!

In **February 2015,** Chelsea reached the **League Cup final** where they beat Tottenham Hotspur 2-0. It was Eden's **second** major **trophy with Chelsea** after the **2013 Europa League.**

2014-15 WAS AN AWESOME SEASON FOR EDEN.

He was voted **PFA Player of the Year**

and, for the second year in a row:

CHELSEA PLAYER OF THE YEAR.

Another one!

CHAPTER 10

EDEN THE ICON

Eden's favourite way to **celebrate** a goal? It was the *KNEE SLIDE*, but in 2018 he was doing it so much, it started to hurt his knees. **So he stopped!**

OUCH!

Hazard is one of the most **famous players in the world.** He's cool and funny, so he's appeared in:

And, in 2020, he replaced **Cristiano Ronaldo** as the **cover star** for the

FIFA VIDEO GAME.

YOU GUYS ARE **SO** BAD.

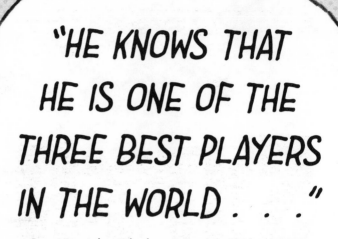

"HE KNOWS THAT HE IS ONE OF THE THREE BEST PLAYERS IN THE WORLD . . ."

Jose Mourinho, Eden's manager at Chelsea, 2015

2015-16 was not a great season for Eden and Chelsea. He had a run of games without scoring a goal and even **missed a penalty!**

But by the following season he was **back on form.** After scoring in the first game of the season, Hazard notched up **17 goals** and **seven assists** in **2016-17.**

BOFF!

2017-18 HIGHLIGHTS

SOME OF EDEN'S BEST GAMES OF THE SEASON.

18 OCTOBER 2017

CHAMPIONS LEAGUE GROUP STAGE

CHELSEA 3-3 ROMA

Eden scored his **first Champions League goal** in more than two years – and then scored another to rescue a draw!

20 JANUARY 2018

PREMIER LEAGUE

BRIGHTON 0-4 CHELSEA

The first of Hazard's **TWO** goals was his **100th in league football** as Chelsea hammered Brighton away from home.

20 JANUARY 2018

PREMIER LEAGUE

CHELSEA 3-0 WEST BROMWICH ALBION

Eden made it **SIX goals** in **SIX games** with his brace against the **Baggies.**

It was the second time that season he scored two against West Brom.

19 MAY 2018

FA CUP FINAL, WEMBLEY STADIUM

CHELSEA 1-0 MANCHESTER UNITED

*Chelsea had **lost** the FA Cup final to **Arsenal** in **2017**. It would be different this time!*

Eden picked up a great long ball and ran straight towards goal. United defender **Phil Jones** brought him down in the box.

PENALTY!

Who else would take it but **Hazard,** of course!

With a little step, he sent **David de Gea**
the wrong way and ***BOINK!***

A BRILLIANT PENALTY!

TWACK!

EDEN'S GOAL *WON* THE
FA CUP FOR CHELSEA!

The **2018-19** season was one of Eden's **best ever.** He scored **21 goals** and made **17 assists.**

HE SCORED A **HAT-TRICK** AGAINST CARDIFF CITY!

The **highlight** of the season was the **Europa League** final. Eden scored two goals as **Arsenal** were beaten **4-1.**

This was Eden's last match for Chelsea.

HAZARD'S CHELSEA RECORD

SEASON	GAMES	GOALS	ASSISTS
2012-13	62	13	24
2013-14	49	17	10
2014-15	52	19	13
2015-16	43	6	8
2016-17	43	17	7
2017-18	51	17	13
2018-19	52	21	17
TOTAL	352	110	92

Eden is ninth on the list of Chelsea's

ALL-TIME TOP SCORERS.

Hazard scored or assisted a goal every

132 minutes for Chelsea.

"AFTER MESSI AND RONALDO, HAZARD IS MY FAVOURITE PLAYER. I LOVE WATCHING HIM BECAUSE HE IS A PLAYER WHO CREATES THINGS AND IT IS OFTEN SPECTACULAR TO SEE HIM PLAY."

Zinedine Zidane

CHAPTER 12

THE REAL DEAL

In the summer of 2019, Eden said goodbye to Chelsea and signed for the mighty

REAL MADRID.

The transfer fee was an estimated

£90 MILLION

50,000 fans welcomed him at the **Bernabéu stadium!**

Eden was going to wear the famous **number 7** shirt, like **Cristiano Ronaldo.**

HEY, NICE SHIRT!

119

Hazard had supported **Real Madrid** as a boy. Mainly because his hero, **Zinedine Zidane** played there.

Now Zidane was his manager at Madrid!

Eden could hardly believe it.

WOW!

HONOURS AND AWARDS

JUST SOME OF THE TITLES AND AWARDS WON BY HAZARD.

LIGUE 1 WINNER
2010-11

COUPE DE FRANCE
2010-11

PREMIER LEAGUE
2014-15
2016-17

FA CUP WINNER
2017-18

EUROPA LEAGUE
2012-13
2018-19

PFA PLAYER'S PLAYER OF THE YEAR
2008-09
2009-10
2014-15

QUIZ TIME!

How much do you know about **Eden Hazard?** Try this quiz to find out, then test your friends!

1. How many brothers does Eden have?

   ----

2. Which club did Lille sign Eden from?

   ----

3. Which French player did Eden idolise?

   ----

4. Which team did Eden score a hat-trick against in his final game for Lille?

   ----

5. How many goals did he score for Lille in total?

----

6. What was Hazard's estimated transfer fee when he signed for Chelsea?

----

7. How many times did he win the Premier League?

----

8. How many goals did Eden score at the 2018 World Cup?

----

9. Which team does Hazard's brother Thorgan play for?

----

10. How many assists did Hazard provide in his final season at Chelsea?

The answers are on the next page *but no peeking!*

ANSWERS

1. Three
2. Tubize
3. Zinedine Zidane
4. Nancy
5. 50

6. £32 million
7. Two
8. Three
9. Borussia Dortmund
10. 17

EDEN HAZARD:
WORDS YOU NEED TO KNOW

Premier League
The top football league in England.

PFA
Professional Footballers' Association.

Coupe de France
The top French knockout cup competition.

FA Cup
The top English knockout cup competition.

Ligue 1
The top football league in France.

UEFA Champions League
European club competition held every year. The winner is the best club team in Europe.

ABOUT THE AUTHORS

Simon's first job was at the Science Museum, making paper aeroplanes and blowing bubbles big enough for your dad to stand in. Since then he's written all sorts of books about the stuff he likes, from dinosaurs and rockets, to llamas, loud music and of course, football. Simon has supported Ipswich Town since they won the FA Cup in 1978 (it's true - look it up) and once sat next to Rio Ferdinand on a train. He lives in Kent with his wife and daughter, two tortoises and a cat.

Dan has drawn silly pictures since he could hold a crayon. Then he grew up and started making books about stuff like trucks, space, people's jobs, *Doctor Who* and *Star Wars*. Dan remembers Ipswich Town winning the FA Cup but he didn't watch it because he was too busy making a Viking ship out of brown paper. As a result, he knows more about Vikings than football. Dan lives in Suffolk with his wife, son, daughter and a dog that takes him for very long walks.